# Eco-minimalism
## the antidote to eco-bling

C000163239

RIBA ⸬ **Publishing**

© Howard Liddell, 2013

Published by RIBA Publishing Ltd
15 Bonhill Street, London EC2P 2EA

ISBN 978 1 85946 495 3

Stock Code 80357

The right of Howard Liddell to be identified as the Author of
this Work has been asserted in accordance with the Copyright,
Design and Patents Act 1988, Sections 77 and 78.

All rights reserved. No part of this publication may be
reproduced, stored in a retrieval system, or transmitted, in any
form or by any means, electronic, mechanical, photocopying,
recording or otherwise, without prior permission of the
copyright owner.

British Library Cataloguing in Publications Data

A catalogue record for this book is available
from the British Library.

Author: **Howard Liddell**

Commissioning Editor: **Lucy Harbor**

Project Editor: **Neil O'Regan**

Designed by **Kneath Associates**

Printed and bound by
**WG Baird Ltd, Antrim**

We make every effort to ensure the accuracy and quality of
the information when it is published. However, we can take no
responsibility for the subsequent use of this information, nor for
any errors or omissions that it may contain.

RIBA Publishing is part of RIBA Enterprises Ltd.

www.ribaenterprises.com

Cover photo: **Michael Wolchover,**
Glentress Visitor Centre by Gaia Architects

# contents

# Foreword

*By Robin Harper*

I cannot work up much enthusiasm for designs that are 'award-winning' and 'innovative' unless there is a positive answer to the question 'but does it work'? If buildings reflect their zeitgeist then that might explain why 20th century 'green buildings' were often applauded but usually proved to be phoney. The difficulty is that, of all the things that might be associated with a building, its impact on the physical environment is, well, physical. This book goes straight to the heart of the issue.

There is surely no need to rehearse the environmental problems that face the 21st century. We need do no more than flick through the Brundtland Report of 1987 that launched the term 'sustainable development' into the public discourse. None of the environmental problems listed there have been 'solved'. Others like climate change and fresh water scarcity have joined the list.

A building's form can express our concern, may be even our quiet panic, at the emerging crisis – but what emerges is not so much 'eco-home' as 'eco-hospice'. Given that buildings are the point of consumption and impact of about half of society's problematic flows of materials and energy, that iconographic design philosophy is an uneasy, if not inconsistent, perspective. Indeed substituting substance by image risks making everything so much worse. At the tipping point we would have deluded ourselves for so long that the underlying problems have moved from chronic to acute and our only strategy left is one of denial until Mephistopheles arrives.

In terms of reducing the physical impact of buildings, the last decades have disappointed but have not been entirely wasted. The palette of technologies that could be deployed has been assembled. But what has been lacking is a commitment to learn from feedback and urgently regroup. This book is an important step.

As Howard Liddell writes, 'Mechanical engineers can only work with what the architect gives them'. That is why, as President of the Chartered Institution of Building Services Engineers, I am happy to offer this Foreword. Moving to address the physical impact of the building, we are forced to take a systems perspective. A page of tick box-free standing issues won't do. To me Eco-minimalism is a natural consequence of a systems approach. The text raises some big issues for debate. For example it will often require professionals to work in collaboration rather than sequence. But I hope we do not debate for too long because this fine book is aimed to set us off to be effective. Hopefully just in time.

**David Fisk**
Hons FRAEng, FCIBSE FRIBA (Hons)

Aerial truss at Glentress Visitor Centre, Tweed Valley Forest Park.
Photo Howard Liddell

# Preface

The idea for this book dates from the turn of the century (20th/21st). The first article on the topic, for which I dreamt up the seemingly unlikely title of 'Eco-minimalism', was published in 2002 in the SEDA[1] quarterly magazine. I then linked up with Nick Grant, a like-minded co-member of AECB[2], for a joint article in their journal the following year.

The article was intended for the 'green insider' architects and builders (SEDA and AECB members) as a warning that if we didn't confront some harsh 'triple bottom line' realities and crunch some numbers, then our missionary zeal would be undermined by the sceptics who would.

Firstly, I found the approach was anything but a mere insider's critique. It had mileage out on the platforms of every conference centre and community-hall gathering I attended for the ensuing year and, evidently, its message was bridging the gap between the 'green-realists' and the 'every person' on the Clapham omnibus.

Secondly, I forgot where I came into this whole game 30 years ago – through 'alternative technology' – and that when green eventually became cool (about five years ago in the UK), the novice converts followed the same path and were less likely – not more – to crunch numbers than the OAP greenies. Our cries of 'Well we did this back in the 70s and ...' went unheeded as a new, self-confident but blinkered generation insisted on reinventing the green technological wheel.

So the need for this piece of work was in 2008 just as pressing as I had originally thought – and perhaps even more so, but for a different set of reasons.

As I amend this second edition it is alarming to realise that the challenge has become even more urgent – the extent of greenwashing with eco-bling has spread like wildfire and clearly this message has not yet penetrated.

**Howard Liddell**
*Gaia Architects, Edinburgh*
February 2013

1 Scottish Ecological Design Association.

2 Association of Environmentally Conscious Building.

One of many trusses for Glentress Visitor Centre for Forestry Commission. Whilst the timber is from the forest only metres away, after milling, stress grading, prefabrication, storage and then eventually craning into place its embodied energy (through travel over the length and breadth of Scotland), makes a mockery of using local materials.
Photo Howard Liddell

# Acknowledgements

In terms of the Bruntland definition of sustainability – providing for the needs of the present generation without compromising those of future generations – I hope my children will forgive being deprived of their rightful amount of quality father-time whilst I have tilted at windmills, vainly seeking planetary improvement. If so, thanks to them, and to their much-loved Granny Alys – my late mother – who wasted nothing, recycled everything, adored simplicity and was damn good company. Thanks, also, to Auntie May for saying: "A day without learning is a day wasted."

As for those from whom I have been learning daily – as this is my first major book, I get the opportunity to thank 30 years' worth of 'fellow green travellers' for their influence, company and (always the most welcome) humour. Indeed, my epiphany into green buildings came about in 1973 through witnessing the knockabout act of an architect duo called Streetfarmers – so, thank you Graham Caine and Bruce Haggart for not being earnest yet having impact. Those early days included many others who became friends and who contributed significantly to my coursework and research group at Hull School of Architecture, where I was learning far more than the students. Amongst the many are: John Seymour, Peter (Jake) Chapman, Robert and Brenda Vale, Gerry Smith, Ken Yeang, Peter Schmid, Kees Duijvestein and staff and student colleagues, Michael Lloyd, Jim Low, Michael Wheeler, Ian Tod, Geoff Whittleston, Per Gustaffson, Dave Hodges, Andy McKillop, Judy Appleby, Clive Watterson and Robin Baker (at Gaia 1993 to 2009).

From the days of my professorship at Oslo (1979–82) until now, I have continued to learn important stuff from those students and colleagues who gave birth to Gaia Architects in 1984: Chris Butters, Frederica Miller, Dag Roalkvam, Wenche Ellingsen, Bjørn Berge, Rolf Jacobsen and Marianne Leisner. Since 1989, when Bjørn and I decided to set up Gaia International, I have been privileged to work with, and learn a whole heap from, Joachim and Barbara Eble, Rolf Messerschmidt, Declan and Margrit Kennedy, Peter Schmid, Gabriella P'al, Eva and Bruno Erat, Varis Bokalders, Paul Leech, Sally Starbuck, Kimmo and Maritta Kuismaanen, Herbert Dreiseitl, Walter Unterreiner and many more beyond the UK.

I must also thank Nick Grant for his shared interest in eco-minimalism; he was collecting what he called 'limes' (green lemons) at the same time as I was collecting eco-clichés, and this process encouraged us to write a joint article on the subject. Meanwhile, as well as those mentioned elsewhere, Bill Bordass, Paul Woodville, Barbara Chapman, Kathryn Robinson and John Gilbert have helped keep me from my worst rhetorical excesses with some cold, hard facts as well as good debate.

There is, in fact, a whole book, waiting 'in the wings' to be written, about those who have been influential in the sustainable development world over the past 40 years and earlier – many of whom I have been very privileged to meet and talk with. These include Richard Buckminster Fuller, E. F. Schumacher and, now a personal and much-respected friend, George McRobie

– all of whom have inspired with their passion as much as their wise words. I am particularly grateful to George and also to David Fisk for agreeing to contribute some words for me at the beginning and end of this polemic. And special thanks go to Matthew Thompson for his patience and humour and our endless games of email 'tag'. Only he and I shall ever know which words of his were slipped into the text, but I was pleased to be a party to his own modest authorship ambitions.

I owe so much to my 'partner in business and my partner in life',[3] Sandy Halliday, that there is no start or finish. Sandy came into my life at what I hoped would be its halfway stage, and transformed just about everything in it. She has been the sounding board, other half of a '365/7' dialogue and balanced critic for every thought and brainstorm idea I have had over the past 17 years – to the point where I often can't remember the individual source of many of the ideas about which I now write. For her influence on my world I am eternally grateful, and to her influence on this book I pay enormous tribute.

However, I take full and personal responsibility for any inaccuracies, errors or omissions in the script. I have sought to amend a few in this second edition, however, I am sure that every reader will find something to question and, indeed, quietly hope so – as this will mean that the text has been truly read, and that will be thanks enough for the effort expended in putting it together.

**Howard Liddell**
*Gaia Architects, Edinburgh, 2013*

3 Return quote
from *Sustainable
Construction* by
Sandy Halliday.

# Introduction

'Man is far too
clever to be able
to survive without
wisdom'

E. F. Schumacher

The £2 million Glencoe Visitor Centre in the Scottish Highlands.
Photo Howard Liddell

The original motivation for this book was based on the desire to avoid a feeling of déjà vu. Many of us have been here before – anyone old enough to remember the OPEC oil price rise crisis of 1973 will also faintly recall the rush to all forms of alternative energy as a panacea for solving the world's problems. We raced to construct (and, fortunately, also to monitor) every device – literally – under the sun, and wind, and wave, and tide (lunar power!). In certain circumstances, some of these solutions even worked – and people were encouraged to develop them further, despite the appalling lack of funding. After all, this was the realm of a few hippies and 'environmentalists'. Even now the term 'environmentalist' still carries with it a sense of disparagement. Funny, really: we thought that everyone should have a (positive and inquisitive) interest in 'the hand that feeds us', i.e. the environment.

For many of us, this technical pursuit was also a 'shop window' fronting a comprehensive store of healthy 'pro-planet' and yet pro-development thinking. The 'S' word – sustainability – had not yet come into play, whereas now, of course, it replaces commas in sentences and is used so often in the wrong – or over-simplistic, or one-dimensional – context. As little as 5 years ago the commercial world would freeze at the thought of hinting that anything might be 'eco-friendly', whereas now 'eco-' is a pre-fixation; sadly it routinely green washes an existing and very ungreen product, where only the sales rhetoric has been changed.

How sad it is to have had to watch a new generation not doing their homework. Not finding out what has and has not worked in the past – and more importantly why. Over these past few years I have had to observe the Merton Rule and its even worse offspring the Scottish Climate Change Act making mandatory useless micro-renewable devices and then – even worse – seeing governments skewing this unyielding energy field with farcical fiscal incentives in order to support inherently unworkable micro-technologies, which are then promoted by gangs of ruthless doorstepping carpetbaggers. At the time of writing the so-called 'Green Deal' is still being launched. It is already being called the 'Green Sub-Prime', because it has more to do with arranging loans (at 7% Pa interest) than resolving net energy bills (and also uses some optimistic assumptions on what will be delivered). The tragedy is that not only will it never take a single family out of fuel poverty, it will most likely make things worse.

# 'It's not personal'

St George's School, Wallasey, is the UK's earliest purpose-designed solar project. It was later monitored and compared to an equivalent neighbour school. It was found that 30 per cent of the reductions were down to the solar gains and the rest to low ventilation, the occupants and high-wattage lighting.
Architect Emslie Morgan 1965. Photo Howard Liddell

**The Streetfarmers were a green direct action student architect group, who built their self-sufficient eco-house for £1,500 in the grounds of South Bank Poly and lived in it for 18 months.**
Architects Streetfarmers 1974. Photo Howard Liddell

**An early and simple, passive Eco-house was built in the suburbs of Stockholm by Bengt Warne in 1977. The living quarters were on the first floor, the bedrooms and ablutions in the cellar and the garden under glass on the roof.**
Architect Bengt Warne. Photo Howard Liddell

It seems that the common response to the realisation that climate change and a concern for the environment are not luxury issues is to take a global perception and then make a highly personal response. We recycle cans, bottles and paper in the office, build an eco-extension, draught-seal an existing dwelling, and so on. Maybe it is because the requisite effective action is at a level so immense that it is necessary to start with what an individual can control, i.e. their own life and behaviour. There is a basic need, born of frustration, to do SOMETHING.

However, it is in our community, professional, commercial and political activity that we can make the most impact: moving on from the 'autonomous' house to the low-impact community and, in the case of the designing and constructing professions, to the delivery of what they design and build. The impact of an architect half-filling the office kettle is of miniscule significance set beside the specification of an airtight and highly insulated building, which will also save a lot of money for the building users and reduce its carbon footprint ('win–win').

And so it was in the 1970s (in the case of Wallasey School, the 1960s) that, looking beyond their personal behaviour, a whole raft of experimenters (with dress codes ranging from green boiler suits at the Streetfarm to Savile Row suits or brown corduroy at the Cambridge Autarkic House) built things of very varying prices and with equally varying degrees of success. But they built, and that was important, so that we could learn what worked and what didn't.

It is therefore with a sense of utter frustration that (40 years on) I have had to watch the pre-emptive publicity for eco-developments by certain companies, only then to fall prey to the reality of the actual performance of the moving parts, and the damaging publicity not just to these projects but to the whole momentum of eco-building in their wake.

It is not always clear why something was successful, but it is usually pretty obvious why something failed. In an age of obsession with risk assessment, it is difficult enough to get the opportunity and resources to experiment and therefore doing our homework from precedents – however far back they go – is crucial.

# Learning from the past

'Things should be as simple as possible – but no simpler'

Albert Einstein

The 1970s TV programme *A House for the Future* was a response to its contemporary political situation, which came in the wake of the OPEC action – seen at the time as an 'energy crisis'.

Inevitably, the focus of the programme was on energy and energy technology, but its demonstration building did get the basics – airtightness and high insulation levels – right, and it did also involve the hands-on Grant family: one of the very first 'reality TV' families. In the final two programmes, it also looked at the wider picture – including the author's solar terraces project in Hull.

For a television programme, the most important aspect was that it should be visual and engage the interest of the audience. For the Grant family, and all those involved in the building, the conversion of their 'green' house (a product) into a 'sustainable' way of life (a process) was of much more significance.

Geoff Grant was very handy and technically competent, and he and his family kept very good records of the house in use. In going back to the project one year later, with some of the students who helped in the building, we learned a great deal.

In the illustration below is a list of the key eco-technologies used in the house. Over the 13 weeks of the programme, one technology/topic per week would be the focus of attention. Highlighted in red are the ones that really worked.

Once its energy demand had been brought down, the majority of the supply-side technologies were redundant and the whole house could effectively be heated by casual gains from the family, equipment, lights and – especially – by heat recovery from the kitchen.

The simple lesson?
To look at lowering the demand for energy in the first place, before getting excited about alternative energy technology on the supply side of the equation. And save a lot of money and hassle.

Granada TV 1976 – *A House for the Future*. The conversion of a brick barn in Macclesfield into an eco-house. The selected family got volunteer help – including from the author and Hull architecture students.
Producer Brian Trueman.
Architect Don Wilson 1976.
Photo Howard Liddell

## What worked?

- **High insulation levels**
- **Airtight skin**
- **Active solar roof**
- **Passive solar greenhouse**
- **Rock store under greenhouse**
- **Heat pump**
- **Wind turbine**
- **Heat recovery from kitchen**
- **Energy saving fittings**
- **Low emb. energy materials**
- **Allotment garden**
        **etc, etc**

# UK Design Award for a house that happened to be green

Back in the late 1980s, Peter and Marjorie Bourne, a Perthshire artist and teacher respectively, did not want a standard kit house but an architect-designed house. However, they wanted it on a budget not dissimilar to that of a kit house – a tall order, but that was the brief.

Any technical-fix add-ons would almost certainly have ended up being taken off at the final pre-construction budget check.

The preliminary concepts started, therefore, with a passive design approach, and the envelope had airtightness and insulation levels as high as was considered worthwhile at the time. It worked well with a single 5 kW wood-burning stove heating the whole of its 160 m² floor area.

The two-storey house was designed with a south-facing (passive solar) stairwell, with four half levels, and the building was completed for a cost of £86,000 in 1992. The clients were offered twice that price for the house on the day they moved in.

In dealing with passive solar gain, the building also addressed wider lighting issues – particularly so that the clients could continue with their painting. It was also

a house which they found very healthy, and they talked about the positive impact of the smell and the colour of the natural wood and breathable (moisture transfusive) mineral-paint finishes.

The project fought a few battles – actually because (a) it was not like a standard (timber-frame) kit house and (b) because it was clad in timber externally. It started on a separate site in 1989, and, owing to Planning Department resistance to it being granted permission, was finally built in the back garden of the client's former home and handed over in 1992.

In 1995, and after the house had acquired a number of awards, the local authority, who had resisted the project for nearly two years, included it in their handbook as an exemplar of how to build houses in the countryside.

Twenty-two years later Gaia Architects has repeated this achievement with a Scottish House of the Year Award for Architectural Excellence 2012. The fact that it is the first Brettstapel Passivhaus in the UK appeared to have passed the notice of the judges.

Plummerswood is the first Brettstapel (dowelled mass timber), certified Passivhaus in the UK and won the Architectural Excellence award for Scotland's House of the Year 2012 image Sandy Halliday.

Tressour Wood House for Peter and Marjorie Bourne was the UK House of the Year 1993, a Design Award for a house that happened to be green. No bells or whistles – just simple passive design.
GAIA Architects 1992.
Photo Colin Wishart

# The Four Elements

To live comfortably we need to deal effectively with four elements: Air, water, earth (materials) and fire (energy)

We humans have only been out of the caves and constructing our own habitat in the open for about 10,000 years. Termites got there well before us, and have been building for over 200 million years.

Apart from controlling temperature with earth, part of the sophistication of the termite mound is the way in which its walls 'breathe'– the way that they deal with moisture and air passively – and all this without technology, merely using intuitive, very well applied science.

Our tendency through the 20th century was to rely increasingly on technology to deal with air and moisture in our buildings, whereas we used to allow the building fabric to cope with this.

We have also come to depend ever more on technology for processed, composite and artificial building materials and for our energy supply and equipment.

My practice, GAIA, has developed an approach to design which seeks to close the loops on all these four elements (as shown opposite), in the interests of pursuing good science, before reaching for increasingly over-engineered and often inappropriate technological solutions.

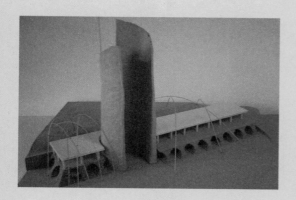

**A project using materials as termites and nest-builders do – for a proposed Centre for Animal Architecture.**
Architect Gaia 2004. Photo and model Icosis

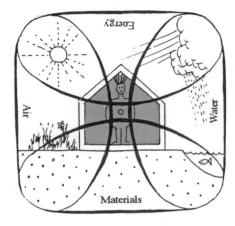

The way we came to build in the 20th century disregarded not just where goods and services came from and where they went to at the end of their usage 'cycle', but even the impact they could have on human comfort and human habitat whilst incorporated in buildings.

Image Bjørn Berge

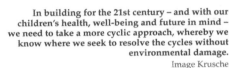

In building for the 21st century – and with our children's health, well-being and future in mind – we need to take a more cyclic approach, whereby we know where we seek to resolve the cycles without environmental damage.

Image Krusche

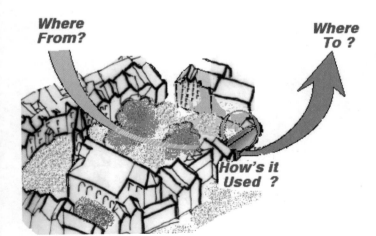

**'Where is it from? How is it used? Where does it go?'**

Instead of having a linear flow of the four elements, we seek to have a cyclic flow. This is about knowing where something comes from, knowing how to use it well – in other words, using it to its maximum potential – and knowing where it will go to at the end of its functional life.

Just as this construct has been used successfully in ecological building design, so it has been used as an organising principle for the two core chapters of this book.

In working with groups of 10-year-olds on their utopian eco-cities we have developed a simple set of rules. They need to know where the four elements for their buildings come from, where they go to at the end of their useful life and how they work when incorporated into buildings.

Image Howard Liddell

'The system of nature, of which man is a part, tends to be self-balancing, self-adjusting, self-cleansing. Not so with technology.'

E. F. Schumacher

# eco-bling

Tuscan sunrise. Photo Howard Liddell

# fire

element

# Photovoltaic Solar Cells

The triumphant power of electricity and its attendant gadgetry was much trumpeted in the 1920s as something which would 'free the housewife from drudgery', and indeed it did. It has created a love affair with all things electrical ever since and it was the 20th century's 'sexy' energy supply. It was even perceived as clean.

As we have evolved into the electronic age and especially since the advent of the solar-powered calculator, there has been an optimistic industry developing an optimistic body of potential customers transfixed by the promise of electrical power from the sun through photovoltaic solar cells.

But electricity generation has always had a major drawback – it is bound to be more expensive than the oil, coal, gas and nuclear sources that, predominantly, it exploits for its creation by comparison with using those same fuels directly. In other words, the direct energy from burning oil, for example, will always be cheaper than the cost of electricity generated from burning oil. Solar-energy supply to a consumer is no different: like any basic fuel, it is only as cheap as the cost of exploiting it for an end use.

In the case of photovoltaic cells, the hope has always been that the exploitation cost would drop rapidly with increase in demand, and that economies of scale would kick in.

Since the first edition of this book two things have happened. The first is the very rapid establishment of a photovoltaic industry and a small but still not yet significant reduction in costs. The second is a scheme called FITs (Feed-in Tariffs) in which the Cameron Government saw 'fit' to pay 26p per kW for photovoltaic-generated electricity – or twice the cost for consumers to use it. This is clearly unsustainable and the efforts now are to pull this back. This does not mean that there is no precedent for this kind of fiscal action because we have all been subsidising nuclear power since the 1950s, and will continue so to do in perpetuity.

(Nuclear fusion was once promised as 'too cheap to meter'. Subsequently there was also the tantalising (but unrealised) promise in the 1950s of the abundance of nuclear fission.)

We need to have transparency about exactly how much these various energy technologies are providing and at what cost (both financially and environmentally) – and which ones we are prepared to subsidise and which ones we are not – and, most importantly, why.

Photovoltaics seem almost
magic – they turn sunlight
into electricity.

But it takes rather a lot of
photovoltaic cells to make
not very much electricity.

This top floor of an otherwise (primarily) passive and low carbon four-storey block of academic offices has 34kW of photovoltaics feeding a building where the all-glazed room itself has a heating demand greater then 34kW. The array has also failed after 3 years and requires total replacement.
ZICER building, VEA. Photo Howard Liddell

# Heat Pumps

The closed-loop ground source heat pump (GSHP) is the most common geothermal technology in the UK. They are most efficient when producing the low temperatures required for underfloor heating. Manufacturers claim that a good-quality system operating in these circumstances should give a coefficient of performance (COP) of approximately 4. In other words, 1 kWh of electricity is used to displace 4 kWh of heat. In reality most seem to have seasonal COPs in the region of 2.5 to 3, and not 4 upwards as manufacturers claim, and are likely to be nearer 2.5.

A heat pump (like that at the core of most modern fridges, for example) exploits the property of certain 'phase-change' chemicals to extract or expel heat as they convert from liquid to gas (and produce freezing conditions at the other side of the system in the process – hence, the fridge). The gas is then repeatedly compressed back to a liquid by a compressing pump driven by electrical energy.

However, electricity costs more than other fuels per unit of energy output because it is a secondary source of energy supply, produced from a primary fuel (most commonly oil, coal or gas). To make a direct comparison, the example, of a power station that creates electricity using gas is being considered here. Such power stations historically have been unable to exploit the gas at more than 40 per cent efficiency, and averaged out over time their performance has been much lower than this. 'Grid losses' (i.e. the energy lost in transmitting the electricity from power stations along cables to the end user) run at about 8 per cent, and when these are added it is clear that electricity in our homes is delivered very inefficiently when referring back to the primary fuel from which it is derived – in this case, gas.

The differential in tariffs between one unit of gas and one equivalent unit of electricity is around three to one. Given that this is about the same as the average output efficiency of a heat pump – i.e. about three units out to one unit in – it seems like an awful lot of technical complication, expense and effort to get back to where we started. One unit of gas, which could have been used directly in the first instance in a 97 per cent efficient domestic condensing boiler, arrives instead in a heat-pump supply system as derived energy from a long journey – via a rank of industrial gas boilers, a hall of turbines, miles and miles of national grid and, finally, a domestic heat pump as one-quarter to one-third of a unit of electricity.

Against oil the figures stack up better.

The impact of GSHPs can be more favourable:

> in all-electric buildings (where grid electricity is being displaced, instead of gas);

> where the electricity is from an on-site renewable source (however grid connected renewables are not $CO_2$ neutral and they are very expensive compared to purchasing from a renewable source);

> where the pump is used to provide cooling in the summer as well as heating in winter (not something we wish to encourage).

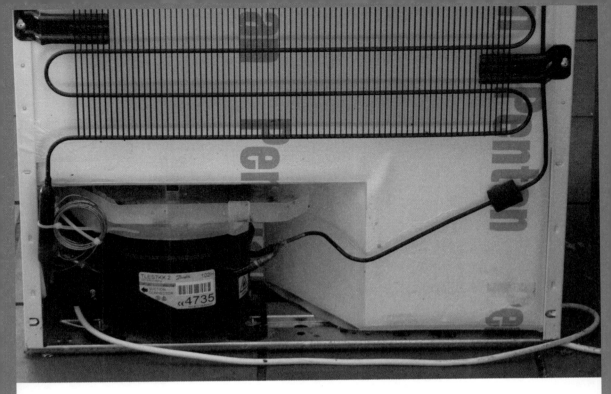

Most houses have a version of a heat pump – at the back of the fridge. It uses freon which absorbs heat (from food and drink) when changing phase from liquid to gas. The heat is then rejected as the pump compresses the gas back to liquid.

Photo Howard Liddell

The equipment: one energy unit in – three units out.

The energy supply: electricity costs three times as much as the gas that generated it.

Result: an exercise in technological redundancy.

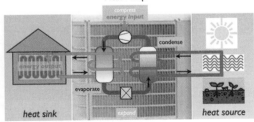

**Heat Pump**

compress
energy input

condense

evaporate

expand

heat sink

heat source

# CHP (Combined Heat and Power):
## Balancing Hot Water and Electricity.

Hot air emerging from a power station's cooling towers following condensation inside seems to signal waste. To exploit waste heat more effectively and use it for making hot water appears, clearly, to be a better option. However, it is how this secondary exploitation can be used that presents the challenge.

Whilst the demand for electricity and for domestic hot water is relatively constant, the round-the-year demand for hot water for space heating is not. The only way this can work efficiently is if the hot water requirement of the total system is constant (e.g. round-the-clock and year-round, such as for a hospital or swimming pool).

In most situations, the overall summer hot water demand of a building will be significantly lower than its overall winter hot water demand. Therefore, if the system has been sized for the maximum loading (in winter), then the hot water coming from the electricity generation process in the summer will need to have somewhere other than a space-heating network to go to – or be jettisoned (e.g. as in a cooling tower).

The other option is to have a CHP system sized on the summer load only, and have an additional system for supplying the extra winter demand. This does, however, mean the installation of two systems rather than one, which will then reduce much of the basic benefit.

There has been much research over the past 30 years into alternative ways of generating electricity that would overcome the above dilemma – such as the (solar-powered) Stirling cycle engine – but, as yet, there is little in the form of applied output.

Using the waste heat from electricity generation for hot water only works with a constant round-the-year demand for hot water.

**The CHP plant black building at Loretto, Tübingen, sits next to the parking machine building and is powered by gas and biofuel.**
Architects Tübingen City Council.
Photo Howard Liddell

# Thermal Solar Collector

This is possibly the oldest 'green badge' technology. Customers often want an obvious outward demonstration of their green intentions, and this shouts it from the rooftops (even if it doesn't move like a wind turbine!).

The thermal solar collector, which basically seeks to heat water directly from the sun, is probably the simplest of all the eco-technologies. If kept simple and if self-built, it can be very cost-effective. For example, a second-hand radiator painted black with an underlying insulating layer and a sheet of glass over it will heat water from the sun's rays reasonably effectively. If an off-the-peg commercial installation is purchased, then it is likely to be less easy to justify on cost terms.

A very large proportion of the first generation of commercial solar-thermal installations worked technically but not constructionally, and many have not survived long enough to pay back their investment. Whilst longevity has gone up and costs have come down (but not by much) the payback period – without fiscal intervention (e.g. Feed-in Tariffs) – is still relatively long.

In the UK – depending on location – this payback period (the length of time it takes for the capital cost of the equipment to match the value of the energy obtained over time from the sun) is usually quoted at around 12 to 15 years.

A paradox exists, whereby the more one pays for the quality of the solar-thermal apparatus, the longer the payback period. This is because there is insufficient difference in energy efficiency between a simple home-made collector and a sophisticated top-of-the-range commercial product.

In the right place, at the right angle, it will work best on sunny days, and inefficiently on overcast days.

How long is the payback time?

The Centre for Alternative Technology in Wales has been testing out industry-produced thermal solar collectors since 1973.  In terms of cost-efficiency (payback period), none can come close to their home-made versions.

Home-made solar collector.AT. Photo Howard Liddell

# Condensing Boilers:
## Cheap ones don't condense.

Condensing boilers have already been enshrined in the good-practice manuals and are generally regarded as a 'good thing'. Given the relatively small difference in cost between a non-condensing boiler and a condensing unit it seems a perfectly logical choice, and, indeed, in most cases is probably good practice.

Basically, the condensing boiler is designed to burn its gas fuel more efficiently and to give off fewer emissions from the flue. Such a technical provision certainly scores well in government-backed rating schemes such as those required by the Building Regulations, and as a score for BREEAM[4] building assessments.

However, cheap units can fail very quickly – becoming a non-condensing boiler – and unless people invest in quality, they will find that they have merely participated in a cynical 'tick the green box' exercise. After a couple of years, they can end up being no better off than they would be with a conventional boiler.

The context of the installation is also important. Is the building fabric – in its walls, floors and ceilings – energy efficient in the first place? Is there a high level of insulation, and is the building airtight? These issues are important because if the building is constructed to minimum standards (or built below them, as is all too often the case), then the main benefit of a condensing boiler is already lost – and more.

It is also worth having the demand side calculated, because the methods used by many heating installers are rudimentary and often based merely on gross square metreage, irrespective of the energy efficiency of the building envelope. As installers will want to guarantee thermal performance, their estimate will always tend towards the worst-case scenario – and this will doubly penalise energy-efficient homeowners. In the first instance, they will be paying for boilers larger than they need, and, secondly, the units will always be operating at a lower output than is efficient, because boilers work most efficiently when going flat out.

4 Building Research Establishment Environmental Assessment Method.

Cheap boilers often fail
to condense after a
short period.
Oversized installations will
always operate inefficiently.

The author has had disappointing
experience with condensing boilers,
and has learnt that cheap ones often fail
within months.
Photo Howard Liddell

# District Heating

The reasoning behind district heating is that having many buildings connected to a centralised delivery system will produce efficiencies, economies of scale and reduced costs for heating. One central heating boiler system is traded off in cost terms against lots of small individual ones in each building.

The critical issues then become:

> the overall layout of the buildings being supplied (from low-rise, low-density suburbia to high-rise, high-density inner-city buildings);

> the energy efficiency of the individual properties being supplied (and rewards for the most efficient);

> the distance that the hot water in the flow and return pipes needs to travel between properties.

Clearly, the denser a development, the more efficient it will tend to be; therein lies the critical point that precedes any decision-making on such a technology. However, with the privatisation of the energy supply industry and the associated individual rights to change supplier, the consistency over time of the demand, and therefore the long-term viability of such an installation, can look risky.

The intention is efficiency through economies of scale.

The demand needs to be consistent and the distances short for this to be delivered.

In the small and compact village of Blons in a Vorarlberg forest, this woodchip plant feeds all the main community buildings and a significant number of the neighbouring houses. It works here because of the compactness of the village and readily available woodchip.
Photo Howard Liddell

# air

# element

arge Hilltop Turbines. Photo Howard Liddell

# Conservatories

Conservatories are assumed to be an all-round 'good thing' from an energy point of view. It is for this reason that they can be built without the need for Planning or Building Regulation permissions for all locations barring conservation areas[5].

However, any positive benefits – a reduction in wind chill on the external wall against which the conservatory is placed, and free passive solar gains coming through the glass – are of no value if the conservatory is then fitted with a heating system.

Any heating system placed in a conservatory will spend most of its energy heating the sky on the other side of the very high heat loss glass (even if it is double or triple glazed). If the heating appliances are connected to the house central heating system and are not separately zoned, then this already negative situation is exacerbated.

This is a case of the triumph of sociology over technology. People want to be in their glazed spaces in midwinter, and not just on sunny days. A recent survey established that 90 per cent of conservatories have some form of heating system in them. This converts a carbon-saving strategy into a carbon-using one.

Slightly less significant – but still of note – is the fact that there is quite a lot of embodied energy in the glass and the supporting structure of a conservatory. For the first few years of its life (even if it is unheated), the carbon saving delivered by the greenhouse effect will be paying off the energy used in the structure's manufacture and delivery to site. The figure is significantly more if constructed from uPVC rather than timber.

Conservatories were exempted from planning permission on the basis that they would make a positive energy contribution to houses. The reality is the exact opposite.

5 Professor Tadj Oreszczyn, Lecture on Energy Efficiency at Royal Institution, Glasgow, 15 February 2006.

This 1980s Perthshire Conservatory by GAIA has now been fitted out with a jacuzzi and underfloor heating. Not a cheap decision, for the client or the planet.

Gaia Architects 1995.  Photo Howard Liddell

# Small Wind Turbines

The significant and powerful lobby against 'wind turbines on the hill' insists, somewhat disingenuously, that it is not against wind power per se – merely the large wind farms that make a visible impact on the landscape (although it is not usually mentioned that these areas are often already disfigured by geometric patches of heather burning and criss-crossed with pylons). This argument has influenced the move to small wind turbines, taking them off the hills and instead onto buildings – a strategy exacerbated by policies such as the 'Merton Rule' (which demanded a level of 10 per cent on-site renewables). However, the relative cost-effectiveness, efficiency, energy output and even carbon footprint of the two options is very different. A recent study for a 14-house development in Cornwall demonstrated a twofold increase in the capital cost of investing in small-scale as opposed to large-scale turbines, and an increase of a factor of 20 in the energy output by large-scale rather than small-scale turbines[6].

We should learn from the wind turbine manufacturing industry in Germany, which has become discredited for selling grant-assisted small-scale turbines to householders in becalmed areas, who, not unreasonably, have been very unhappy with the performance of their (albeit subsidised) investments. Effective wind exploitation opportunities are very location-specific, and a blanket policy of removing the need for planning permission for small turbines will be both ineffective and rapidly bring wind power into disrepute.

Any discussion of micro-installations is always about grid connection (or not). It is feasible to use wind energy for purposes other than feeding into a 240-volt interface with the national grid – it can go to battery storage, with output into 12- or 24-volt systems or to a heat churn (making hot water through friction from blades attached to a turbine). Alternatively, it can be used to pump water or for some other mechanical, rather than electrical, purpose.

6 Source: Peter Warm Associates.

As builders throughout the centuries have tended to place houses in sheltered locations, it is unlikely that many houses are sitting on a prime wind-turbine site.

Amongst nine highly different experimental houses in Skive, Denmark, this wind-powered version had a heat churn system (for creating hot water). It lasted mere days when the vibrations were found to be excessive.
Various architects 1977. Photo Howard Liddell

# Mechanical Ventilation

If you find yourself having to get away quickly but needing an unavoidable visit to the WC, the post-event hand-washing decision is easy. On the wall there is an automatic 7 kW electrically-powered hand dryer, and next to it a paper towel dispenser. Not only will the paper towel do the job more quickly, it will do it more cheaply, will use orders of magnitude less carbon and, if the sign by the electrical hand dryer in a certain City Council Department of Environmental Health is to be believed, it is also '250 times more hygienic' than using the hand dryer[7].

Fans are reasonably efficient at moving air around, but not very effective at dealing with moisture. There is a very interesting development amongst ecological-design architects, who are using materials that are 'vapour open'. These include untreated timber (especially end grain) hemp/lime and unbaked clay, in either plaster or brick form. When these are left natural – or are treated with mineral or vegetable paints, which are also 'vapour open' (i.e. moisture transfusive) – the ventilation requirement for mitigating humidity is dramatically reduced. There is much anecdotal evidence of mirrors not steaming up in bathrooms in which such materials are used, as the walls/ceilings are acting as a moisture buffer and ironing out the peaks and troughs.

My experience is that mechanical services engineers do not accept hygroscopicity as a relevant factor and will over-specify the ventilation system accordingly.

7 DTU (2005) *Moisture Buffering of Building Materials:* Report BYG°EDTU R-126 from the Department of Civil Engineering, Technical University of Denmark.

Finnish research has shown that hygroscopic (moisture-absorbing) materials are nine times more effective than mechanical ventilation at dealing with indoor humidity.

This kitchen extract system from a brand new BREEAM Excellent - rated building in Scotland makes the author think that the engineers may have taken the (equipment-industry-written) CIBSE Specification Guide too much to heart.

Photo Howard Liddell

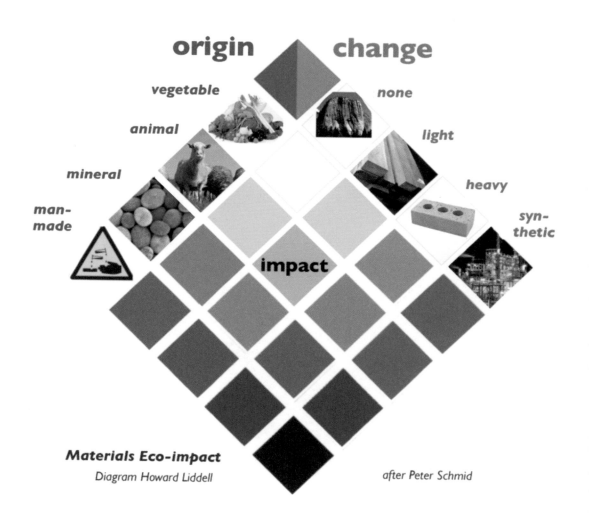

**origin**     **change**

vegetable     none

animal     light

mineral     heavy

man-made     syn-thetic

impact

**Materials Eco-impact**

Diagram Howard Liddell

*after Peter Schmid*

# earth

element

# Green Roofs

The expression 'turf roof' has become a generic term that covers a whole range of different types of planted roof surfaces. Often the term 'green roof' is used instead.

The original Norwegian vernacular tradition involved 30 to 40 cm of earth being thrown up onto a roof and covered with 28 layers of birch bark for waterproofing.

In modern construction, such a strategy of a (literal) earth or turf roof usually depends for its existence on a petrochemical-based damp-proofing membrane and extra structural support. Neither of these elements readily comes to mind as an environmentally sound specification.

There are now a number of patent sedum roof systems, all of which appear to avoid the weight and some of the material problems, and they justify themselves (a) as solar screening for a flat roof membrane and (b) as part of a SUDS strategy for retaining water from the watercourses. However, they often merely camouflage a traditional asphalt roof, and their longevity is yet to be proven.

All of the above lays aside aesthetic considerations as to whether green roofs belie an attitude that any form of human construction is an affront to a natural setting, and that therefore buildings should be hidden away – so that camouflage is a preferable option to a loud-and-proud architecture.

The phenomenon of the turf roof is probably at least one of the images preventing architects – unaware that ecological design is an approach and not a style – from 'going green'. They constitute another superfluous clip-on badge for the undiscerning architectural student, innocent of their 'Hobbitland' aesthetic.

A turf roof is usually heavy and camouflaging a plastic membrane. A sedum option does at least reduce the additional roof load, but still has the look of Middle Earth about it.
Jane Darbyshire & David Kendall Ltd. Photo Howard Liddell

# Recycled Materials

Recycling – commonly a 'catch-all' phrase covering reuse, renewal and recycling – is often one of the first things that a new convert to the green agenda thinks about.

The associated word 'recyclable' is bandied about as if it really meant something. However, is not everything on earth recyclable somehow? (The author has a bottle of whisky for the first person to send in a suggestion of a material or product that cannot be recycled in some form – even plutonium gets recycled!)

The question is one of how easy and safe it is to recycle a material. Some are relatively simple and others near impossible – especially at affordable prices.

It is very easy to establish whether a building has been constructed with recycling in mind in the first place. There are a couple of structures in central London built with innovative 1960s methods that have become causes célèbres, as they are considered virtually impossible to demolish without spraying half of the capital with (post-tensioned) concrete.

Knowing what we know now, nobody in their right mind would invent reinforced concrete as an easily recyclable material. Its demolition is extremely time and cost intensive.

Doing it differently, and in particular cheaply and safely, is a design challenge that the author would like to throw at the industry. To start the ball rolling might I suggest further investigation into timber-reinforced concrete – a development of Brettstapel construction – used in middle Europe, which can span up to 16 metres (see also nail-free construction on page 89).

Recycling is the last resort, because it virtually always requires significant processing and inputs of additional resources in order to transform the recycled material into something both benign and useful.

In observing the dismantling of a not very old flyover, it becomes clear that it was never ever intended to be taken apart, otherwise why would it take so long and be so difficult to take down?

Oslo ex-motorway. Photo Howard Liddell

# Local Materials

In an age of globalisation there is something quaint about the notion of returning to local materials and to local labour.

The assumption is that using local materials is inevitably going to be cheaper because they have not come as far as an imported material, and they will also have reduced embodied energy because they won't have been transported as far. If they cut out a middleman and add value locally then they are certainly to be considered, but even then it can get complicated.

The reality of pursuing this goal in a world wedded to both certification and centralisation means that a whole raft of institutional hurdles can often undermine it. For example, UK timber with a relatively low structural grading might (a) need to be installed using much larger volumes of wood, (b) still need to be taken many miles away from its woodland for stress grading before being returned to its nearby site, (c) have poor weathering properties and (d) is even, ironically, vulnerable to misplaced opportunism by local people with unreasonable financial expectations.

I have lost count of the number of emergency calls I have had from building procurers saying: "I thought I would use my local architect, but he turns out to know nothing about ecological design – can you help?" (It is unethical for an architect to take on a project from a sitting incumbent – so the answer has been only if he/she agrees, which is not very often.)

What if you live in Glasgow and your most abundant local product is a PVC window? What if a client decides to go for a local architect who has no experience of using local materials?

Not everyone is as fortunate as the residents of the Grenoble region, who can dig up – from right under their feet – the perfect raw material for their buildings with just the right amount of sand content for earth building.
Various architects – Domaine de la Terre, Ile d'Abeau, 1993.
Photo Howard Liddell

# Timber Cladding

Many architects acknowledge that timber cladding is the first material they think of when asked to design an environmentally sound building. However, if it is from an unidentified source, or one that makes unverifiable claims to be sustainable (as is the case with a huge amount of tropical hardwood), then it is very questionable whether its pedigree would stand up to scrutiny in terms of a global strategy for sustainable forestry.

On the other hand, if it is a cheap form of timber it will usually be treated – and the ubiquitous treatments, mostly based on CCA (chromated copper arsenic), are decidedly not environmentally friendly. Indeed, the timbers become potential toxic waste from the moment they are treated, thereby causing an end-of-useful-life disposal problem.

Any non-porous surface treatment to timber cladding – such as petrochemical paint or polyurethane varnish – will also prevent the wood from breathing and cause worse weathering and maintenance problems than it would have had if it had been left alone.

Since the first edition of this book there has been an explosion in the specification of both timber cladding and green roofs, thereby confirming my cynicism that camouflage architecture is the industry's response to issues that deserve better consideration and expose the shallowness of the architects who think 'nature can be fooled' with their greenwash.

Like turf roofs, timber cladding is a 'camouflage' material, often used by aspiring green architects with a limited understanding of the issues.

The Austrians love their timber to weather and go black in places. However, they do not do this without attention to longevity: it is merely their taste – not shared by northern Europeans. In the UK such a vision is likely to be the result of poor timber choice.

School in Vorarlberg. Photo Howard Liddell

# water

# element

Water sculpture, Asperg by Herbert Dreiseitl.
Photo Howard Liddell

# Reed Beds

A favourite of architecture students trying to assert their green credentials, the reed bed sits alongside the solar collector and the building-mounted wind turbine as a highly visible green badge, and is part of the ubiquitous 'green box' of clip-on 'eco-bling'.

Where there is an abundance of land and no prospect of connecting to an existing sewerage system, then occasionally a reed bed system (or, more usefully, a 'designed wetland') will be appropriate.

It makes no sense – not even environmental sense – in an urban context with an adjacent sewerage infrastructure and capacity for the outfall.

It should be borne in mind that many reed beds are a form of monoculture (one type of reed) and that it serves primarily to bring aeration to a plant root zone. It usually makes more sense when secondary treatment (e.g. that required after processing in a septic tank) is justified for the system to comprise a range of plants with the capacity to 'fix' or take out different toxins (e.g. heavy metals).

The land requirement for 'black' (solid effluent) sewage treatment is anywhere between 1 and 2.5 m$^2$ per person, which, even at average densities, adds up quite quickly to a large area. Alternative and less land intensive, even more environmentally sound, options are available, and each circumstance needs to be dealt with in its own right.

Reed beds are land-hungry,
and do not present
themselves as a first option
in an urban context.

This reed bed copes with the grey
water from a school. It has an
educational value beyond its cost
viability.
Architects Kent CC.
Brenzett Primary School Kent.
Photo Sandy Halliday

# Grey-water Recycling

It seems quite sensible to replace the conventional mains supply of potable-quality water to flush thirsty WC cisterns with recycled grey water.

On the other hand, in areas where constancy of water supply is not a big issue it may appear an excessive capital expenditure to install secondary plumbing systems alongside the primary systems when this is set against other environmental-specification items that are competing for attention on limited budgets.

If this water is relatively uncontaminated, containing merely a small proportion of soapy deposits, then recycling it seems like an acceptable water conservation strategy.

However, if biological pollution such as urine gets into the system it will require fundamental cleaning, which at the very least is likely to be expensive and inconvenient. Perfectly reasonable technical solutions are often rendered unacceptable in the face of sociological circumstances (accidents in the shower).

Since the last edition the author has been made aware of a project where BREEAM refused to accept rainwater collection as a valid contribution to a swimming pool supply. The powers that be at BREEAM stated categorically that "rainwater collection is for flushing toilets". Aspirant eco-designers have enough jobsworths in the mainstream bureaucracy without having to deal with friendly fire (water).

Recycling shower and wash-hand basin water might not withstand antisocial habits.

The grey-water recycling in this Oxford College was switched off after just a short time when biological impurities were found coming from the student showers, baths and wash-hand basins.

Linacre College. ECD Architects. Photo Henrietta Temple

# 'Living Machines'

There are many municipal sewerage infrastructure systems that are overcapacity to the extent that they prevent further development in their area. In such situations, natural sewerage systems such as reed beds and 'living machines' are often being proposed, and sometimes also implemented in order to allow development to go ahead.

The so-called living machine is the brainchild of John Todd, an American water engineer, and is based on quite sophisticated and intensive aquaculture as a means of treating sewage. Unlike the reed bed, it does not take up a lot of land: it comprises a pumped system that treats water in a sequence of beds with a variety of plants, each 'fixing' or taking out different pollutants.

Whilst such a system has proven technically successful in cleaning the water, it does rely on a significant amount of input energy to run the pumps and maintain adequate temperature. In the case of one small community system in Scotland this expenditure runs to about £500 per week. It has been commented that this is merely trading one environmental problem, sewage, for another: energy.

'You pays your money and you takes your choice.'

Anonymous

The attraction of a 'living machine' sewerage system is that, unlike reed-bed systems, it is land-efficient. It is, however, relatively energy-intensive.

The Living Machine is an intensive self-sufficient sewerage treatment plant. The one illustrated has worked well for a large community in Scotland for two decades. Its environmental credentials are sound apart from one fatal flaw – the high energy cost of pumping water and keeping the right environmental conditions.
Findhorn Foundation.
Photo Howard Liddell

# Embodied Water

We hear much about embodied energy and there are even those who consider the issue to be of the highest importance once energy conservation has been implemented.

This is because the proportional amounts of energy begin to swing from cost in use to first cost.

However, if we regard potable/processed water as a matter of environmental concern then (as with many other – and even more scarce – environmental resources) the issue of embodied water might well be one for serious concern – and inclusion – in any comprehensive eco-labelling method.

In terms of building materials the pecking order goes from concrete at a surprisingly low 2 litres per kilo through timber (20 l/k), steel (40 l/k) and aluminium (88 l/k) to plastic at 185 l/k. (Just ahead of the water footprint of a standard builders' brew cup of coffee at 140 l/k.)

For those seeking to make paper construction a norm the understanding that paper is around 2,000 l/k may present itself as a disincentive.

If carnivores wish to consider the impact of rice at 3,000 l/k then they need also to address beef at 16,000 l/k.

There is much interest to be had on water footprint equations such as one burger = 100 cups of coffee, etc.

In all sorts of ways the idea of experimenting with paper seems to tick quite a few eco-boxes
– with the notable exception of embodied water at 2,000 litres per kilo of end product.

Photo Bill Bordass

# Rainwater Harvesting:
In competing with more economical environmental strategies, this is usually a low priority.

The usual reason for harvesting rainwater at a local, site scale is to replace highly processed, potable mains water, much of which is simply used for WC flushing, with something that has not been expensively prepared for human consumption but is nonetheless perfectly adequate for the job.

Again, as with many of these new technologies, the main deterrent to its use is how much the idea costs to exploit. Most such systems need to run in parallel with the conventional system, and therefore there is a duplication in the cold-water pipework and end fittings. This is bound to involve additional expense, although there can be economies of scale in larger arrangements.

However, not all rainwater needs to be for consumption indoors, and there is a lot of scope for irrigational or ground-watering use – and even potential savings in a 'pipe-free' SUDS context. (SUDS, or Sustainable Drainage Systems, are designed to reduce urban flooding, enhance local water quality, hold rainwater for amenity purposes or encourage local wildlife, and top up groundwater.)

At root all water supplies are rainwater catchments – each site will have its own economies of scale.

Like anything else that seems to be free, rainwater is only as inexpensive to use as the exploitation costs. The cost of a rainwater barrel is relatively low – use in gardens and simple irrigation avoids the costs of filtering and dual plumbing systems.

Photo Howard Liddell

'In technology reality must take precedence over public relations, because Nature won't be fooled.'

Richard Feynmann

# eco-minimalism

Tuscan sunflowers. Photo Howard Liddell

# fire

element

# Passive Solar Energy

Pointing south-facing glazing at the sun and letting it heat up something solid and heat retaining, like a tiled floor or a brick wall, is a phenomenon that will simply happen sunny day in and sunny day out, without wear and tear. Unlike an 'active' solar energy system, passive solar design requires no plumbing or pumps and virtually no maintenance.

It is not magic, and while the 'greenhouse effect' exploited by greenhouses and conservatories means that short-wave radiation goes in and re-radiated long-wave radiation finds it difficult to get out, other forms of heat transfer – conduction (through a material), convection (in the air) and even a degree of radiation (across a space) – all contribute (once the sun has gone down) to a potential for glazing to be a net loser of energy instead of a net winner. Such losses are relatively easy to resolve via shutters or curtains, but this issue does emphasise that with a passive solar strategy the user – not the system – is active, while in an active system the opposite is the case.

In the section on eco-minimalism (page 105) an equivalent phenomenon relating to moisture buffering and related materials choice is described.

The key to exploiting solar
gain is to ensure that it has
somewhere useful to go and
is not a nuisance.

At Ile d'Abeau in France the earth construction acts as a very effective thermal store that is heated as the sun shines through the conservatory. This keeps the structure at an even temperature 24 hours a day.
Architects various. Domaine de la Terre, 1993. Photo Howard Liddell

# Solar Shading:
## Essential if a benefit is not to become a real nuisance.

Pointing south-facing glazing at the sun is fine for heating a building in the heating season, but such a strategy becomes a liability in the summer. Unless external shading or super-ventilation is included in the design, it is likely that there will be overheating and a resultant cooling requirement – such as airconditioning.

Post-rationalisation of past designs often seeks to ascribe to a ubiquitous 'modern' materials palette virtues that might not stand up to scientific scrutiny. Unfortunately, once the sun is through the glass it contributes to the building's greenhouse effect. Internal blinds merely prevent glare and visual discomfort – they do nothing to mitigate heat build-up. Therefore, it is essential that a summer cooling strategy includes external shading – for example through external blinds or brise-soleil.

Solar shading, in the form of brise-soleil, is often applied as mere decoration, adding interest to an otherwise unpromising façade without doing the job it is designed to perform. Such devices feature occasionally even on north elevations, where – certainly in the UK – their contribution to indoor climate control is zero.

# The glass-and-steel dream beloved of modern architects presents a major carbon challenge.

In most circumstances other than in conservatories, the sun can be as much of a problem as an opportunity. It is essential, therefore, to have (external) shading to prevent any unwanted solar gain getting through the glazing.

Ludesch Town Centre.
Photo Howard Liddell

# Low-energy Equipment

When the Chinese Government decided in the late 1970s to supply its whole population with fridges, its less energy-efficient choice of model – made on a marginal capital cost saving basis – resulted in the electricity supply industry having to build a significant number of additional power stations to cope with the extra load.[8]

The choice appears especially strange when one considers the lack of a free market at that time. The option was there to buy a 'job lot' of a specification to the benefit not just of the state but of all comrades.

Energy rating is one of the few areas in which the EU has successfully implemented an energy labelling and savings strategy. Since the first edition of this book, the UK Government has decided that phasing out high energy use light bulbs will not result in the collapse of the consumerist economy – and might even help it.

In the meantime, it virtually always makes cost-in-use sense to buy energy-efficient appliances, and while clockwork radios and torches may seem oddball, they never require a trip to the shops for spare batteries – merely a modicum of human exercise.

The main resistance to low-energy equipment is that it has been sub-par (e.g. low-energy bulbs being slow to start) and lacks quality design input. This is a valid criticism and needs addressing by designers and engineers.

8 Walt Patterson, The Energy Alternative: Changing the Way the World Works, available on http://www.waltpatterson.org/contents.htm

Reducing the demand for electricity by using low-energy equipment is often caricatured as reducing our standard of living. The opposite is actually true – it will give better value for money.

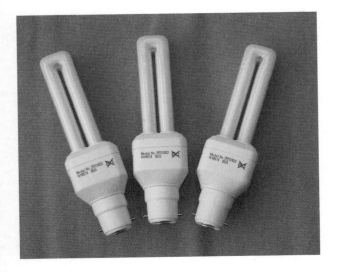

As long as low-energy equipment is optional (and often ugly too), it is unlikely to attract any but the committed greens. Whilst some legislation is a start a lot more commitment and effort is required on the part of (especially lighting) designers to make low-energy equipment more sexy.

Photo Howard Liddell

# Phantom Loads Illus

The introduction of low-energy equipment and dealing effectively with inefficient standby modes can be achieved without threatening personal or corporate standards of living. All that's lacking is the political will to phase in the 'one-watt standby'.

Around 10 per cent of the national electricity grid and 1 per cent of the nation's total energy demand is accounted for by the standby buttons on our electrical and electronic equipment. What is remarkable is that one-watt standby is achievable with currently available technology. Indeed, there is a whole movement seeking to promote such a shift.[9] What is even more significant is that, as with digital television, it could easily be phased in over a very short period as people replaced their equipment. One-watt standby could certainly be achieved in less time than it takes to construct the nuclear power station required to cope with the utterly unnecessary waste caused by inaction on this possibility.

In Australia in 2005, an announcement was made about a strategy for the implementation of a 'one-watt standby' target for appliances, with the potential to save the average household up to AUS$100 per annum and significantly reduce greenhouse gas emissions.

Given that this is an obvious 'win-win' solution, it seems very odd that a strategy to implement such a switch to low-energy standby electronic apparatus is taking so long to introduce to the UK. Because of not having to construct more generating capacity, there is a reduction in the expense of running additional power to the benefit of all.

9 standby.lbl.gov

R · FASTEXT

VIDEO*plus+*

IP / PDC

●REC   ∨ [P] ∧   OTR

⏻   ●REC   ⏱ REC

⏏

While everyone argues about which form of energy is the best for the future – and that the need is urgent – there is a permanent winning card sitting in our hand that we choose not to play. We could very quickly develop across the board 1 W standby equipment instead of the conventional 250 W (plus) that requires us having to build otherwise unnecessary new generating capacity.

Photo Howard Liddell

Equipment sitting on 'standby' mode commands between 8 and 15 per cent of the national electricity grid's demand (estimates vary).

# Renewable Tariffs:
## Defraying the carbon cost of essential electricity.

It is common for clients wishing to 'go green' to look to a domestic-scale solution rather than connecting to a networked system. In generating their own energy, they take both the capital expenditure and the ongoing maintenance on board.

However, each case needs to be taken on its merit. For example, a house-mounted wind turbine is likely, in most locations, to be considerably more expensive per watt generated than a larger, more appropriately sited wind turbine. It will also generate less output per money or carbon unit invested. It will therefore probably have a larger environmental footprint than connection to a network that is exploiting wind where the wind blows rather than in a more sheltered, built-up area.

Every site is different and has its own most appropriate renewable energy source. However, very few plots are capable of efficiently sourcing their own total energy requirement either on-site or close to it. In this circumstance, the option is open either to look to a more appropriate technology or to buy into a renewables tariff from a supplier who already has a low-carbon grid supply network.

A recent client, when informed that a city-centre site was poor for exploiting wind energy, elected to buy into a turbine 100 miles away. Such a direct link was considered necessary within their carbon-neutral marketing strategy.

If a remote source of renewable energy is more carbon-efficient and more environmentally sound in the total calculation than building-mounted renewable apparatuses, does it matter how far away it is?

Reports from 2008/9 investigating a large number of microrenewable sites has indicated that they are working on average at under 8 per cent capacity. If we are to use renewables we must use them efficiently and that will often mean at large scale and centralised.

Zeebruge. Photo Howard Liddell

# Minimum Boilers

Until recently, the minimum size of domestic boiler installation has related to energy-inefficient houses – and was therefore of larger capacity (i.e. 12 kW and above) – and the market had not caught up with a new need for both smaller and more efficient installations. This has meant that the boilers, once they are in an energy-efficient house, are oversized and have been working inefficiently (on and off all the time) or have been causing overheating.

Given that boilers work most efficiently when operating at full load and much less efficiently when on reduced load, there is a clear wastage in both the additional cost of the redundant installed capacity and the economic operation of such systems.

It has only recently become possible to obtain high-ratio turndown boilers (up to 4:1 turndown on their output), an arrangement that allows them to work efficiently at both high output (say, 16 kW) and low output (say, 4 kW).

With the advent of ever-increasing numbers of energy-efficient homes, the further development of purely low-output condensing boilers is to be welcomed (with the caveat of comments made under the section on condensing boilers and their quality, pages 23).

As energy-performance standards increase, the need for large-scale boilers will diminish and, at domestic scale, we will be looking for less-than-5 kW boilers as the norm.

It is only recently that boilers of a sufficient 'turndown' ratio have become available. In energy-efficient homes large boilers will never be able to work flat out and therefore efficiently.
Variable output woodstove in Austrian house.
Photo Sandy Halliday

# Passive House Standard

There is no such thing as a zero-energy building, but we can get close to a zero space-heating building.

The Passive House Standard is defined as a standard of dwelling that cools down by no more than half a degree Celsius over 12 hours and does not require a heating system to provide greater than 10 W/m²/ annum. This might seem quite stringent, but many such houses have been built in northern and central Europe, Scandinavia and Canada for years. There is now a rapidly increasing number being constructed in the UK.

This development should be welcomed in principle, in the context of the poor insulation and airtightness standards that have been prevalent in buildings being constructed in the UK over the past 30 years.

Until very recently new clients very rarely approached an architect's practice asking for a passive house. It is, however, very common for clients to have a strong opinion about supply-side technology – be that a heat pump, a wind turbine, a solar collector or a biomass boiler. The possibility that none of these might be necessary in the first place has not until recently even been part of the public debate.

It should, however, be mentioned that there is a developing concern in Scandinavia about whether the focus on space heating is being overtaken by the rapid expansion in electricity demand – and therefore whether a wider spectrum of issues should be taken on board for overall energy efficiency targets.

There are also other concerns regarding indoor climate issues – these will be addressed in the section on airtightness (page 77).

Since the first edition of this book there has been rapid growth in the interest of Passive House design. In principle, useful, but caution needs to be applied (see under Passive House).

Plummerswood House of the Year 2012 a certified Passivhaus – but with an option to be naturally ventilated (Mechanical Ventilation Heat Recovery can be switched off in favour of manual control, with no evidence of lower annual energy performance.)

Photo Michael Wolchover

Balloon regatta in France. Photo Howard Liddell

# air

element

# Airtightness

It is still the case that the purpose of airtight construction is misunderstood by many who are concerned about its health impacts. An airtight unventilated building does indeed have negative health impacts on its occupants; some air movement is absolutely essential, but the ventilation rate must be controllable and therefore independent of the outdoor wind regime. This is clearly not the case in draughty buildings, but a properly designed airtight building can maintain a consistent ventilation rate in any wind. It is the control and consistency that are important. The mantra is 'build tight and ventilate right'.

Notwithstanding the above there are still many disturbing reports of Passive House buildings that have fanned the flames of the debate with this concern at its core.

## Super-insulation

It only makes economic sense to install super-insulation in a building that is guaranteed airtight. Otherwise the draughts will always win, and the benefit of a reduction in conduction losses through the fabric will not be realised. With both of these in place – and a healthy buildings policy for the indoor climate – a passive standard (minimal input space heating) requirement can often be readily achieved.

## Mandatory MVHR

The most vehement discussions relate to the mandatory nature of MVHR (mechanical ventilation heat recovery) within the process of Passive House (PH) certification. It can be argued that individuals have the option to agree to MVHR and obtain PH certification or opt for the Active House model and go for natural ventilation where control is passed to the responsibility of the user without necessarily having a adverse effect on energy use. Ironically this is no longer an option in Norway, the country of the invention of the Active House concept, where PH certification – and therefore mandatory MVHR – is now inadvisably incorporated into the Building Regulations.

There are important indoor climate issues that follow on from creating an airtight envelope, and this does mean that attention has to be paid to toxicity in internal finishes (adhesives, paints, etc.) and to the ability of the construction to deal with humidity. These matters have not, at the time of writing, been satisfactorily addressed within the PH certification system. We know from monitored buildings across the world that there are serious problems of indoor climate risks, and therefore it is my strongly held view that the PH certificate is falling very far short of the standards it should be promoting.

Without a building being specified, designed and built (and tested) for airtightness, going to higher insulation levels – or even super-insulation – is not sensible, as the vast majority of the heat losses will be through uncontrolled draughts. Placing any form of supply-side energy onto such a building is a waste of money.

Passive standard can only be achieved with guaranteed levels of high insulation and tested and approved airtightness. At the Glencoe Visitor Centre windows were sealed using sheep's wool.

Building and photo Gaia Architects

# Shelter Planting:
## Trees and bushes for energy conservation.

Many projects experience, during late cost-cutting, the removal of landscape elements once they get towards the end of the site operations. Suddenly, trees and bushes do not get planted because they are seen as 'amenity planting' – that is, non-essential decoration.

However, vegetation – or a lack of it – can have a very significant impact, not just on the biodiversity contribution of a development or even as a means of mopping up urban pollutants (which certain shrubs are very good at) but, importantly, on the energy performance of a building.

Trees and shrubs can shelter buildings – especially the elevational areas – from prevailing and chilling winds, with a resultant reduction in heat loss as a benefit. Bushes and trees can also exploit crosswinds, whereby in combination they can induce air to flow over or through rooms needing natural ventilation.

Of course these items have an amenity value – but with a practical (and calculable) economic benefit, they are less likely to be omitted during belt-tightening cost exercises. (These are often referred to as 'value engineering', which, all too often, is in fact merely a capital-cost-cutting exercise.)

# The Finns know about designing for wind shelter: if they get it wrong, drifting snow will block the front door.

Shelter-belt planting can have a significant impact on the energy performance of a development, especially if it protects from cold winter winds, and reduces chill effect. It can also add to outdoor comfort around buildings.
Photo Michael Wolchover

# Natural Ventilation:
Good early design can obviate the need for fans.

The employment of natural ventilation in modern buildings has been happening in experimental structures for quite a while, and client insistence on airconditioning currently appears to be slightly on the wane. There are now a number of high-profile buildings in operation which use the stack effect or atrium design (or both) to draw air through their interiors. In Central Europe and Scandinavia, there are some highly innovative projects using plants, water and natural – or naturally induced – airflows to maintain a comfortable indoor climate.

In Norway, there is even a parent-led initiative for healthy schools using natural ventilation. The thrust for this has emerged from highly positive feedback from a number of pilot schools designed by GAIA Architects in Norway, in the early 1990s.

The search for natural ventilation solutions in larger- scale buildings (without any means of mechanical assistance) has led to some very interesting architectural solutions.
Coventry University. Architect Alan Short. Photo Sandy Halliday

Fan power is more effective at moving air about than dealing with the humidity and pollutants it contains. A return to basic principles can be instructive to designers.

# Natural/hybrid Ventilation

Described here are two examples of innovative methods of natural hybrid ventilation, which whilst based on the principle of natural ventilation sometimes require a boost.

**Culvert cooling (and pre-heating)**

A number of Norwegian schools have been using subterranean ventilation shafts (culverts) for their air intake, in order to obtain a benefit both in summer and in winter from taking up the constant ground temperature (around 10 °C). In winter, this reduces the demand on the heating system by introducing fresh air at a temperature often 20 °C higher than the ambient outdoor winter temperature (on average, consistently well below -15 °C).

In summer, this same process can be used to cool the outdoor air and introduce it into rooms where overheating would otherwise occur. It is sometimes necessary for the stack effect driving this system to need a little fan assistance under low-wind regimes, or in low-rise buildings where a tall enough chimney cannot be engineered simply.

**Dynamic insulation**

Over the past 10 years, a number of buildings in the UK – mostly sports premises or housing – have been designed to maintain their indoor 'climate' (a combination of temperature, humidity and air movement) via dynamic-insulation (also known as 'pore-ventilation') methods. Air is drawn into a room from above the ceiling through a fine membrane and the layer of ceiling insulation. As this air enters the room (through the whole ceiling area), almost as a fine, slow-moving aerosol – it has already taken up the heat that was going out through the ceiling and has also dehumidified the incoming air (warm air holds water more easily than cold air). While the natural stack effect at the extract end can be used to induce the air to go through the membrane, this system usually comprises both a (very-low-wattage) input and output fan. The pressures required to drive the system are orders of magnitude less than those required for conventional mechanical ventilation.

GAIA has pioneered a number of hybrid ventilation techniques in the UK, notably the use of dynamic insulation and culvert ventilation in leisure centres. These are based on the principles of natural ventilation but often require a little bit of low fan power assistance.

BREATHE project. Architects Rotherham City Council. Ventilation and materials consultants Gaia. Photo RCC

Earth arches, New Guerna by Hassan Fathy. Photo Howard Liddell

Earth arches at the Valley of the Kings, Luxor Egypt. Photo Howard Liddell

# earth

element

# Biodiversity

There are many benefits at all levels – whether local, regional or global – in seeking to increase the biodiversity of all built-environment projects.

The tendency in cities has been for green areas to be set apart rather than integrated – for example, as parks – and even then they tend to comprise swards of grass and set piece flower arrangements in preference to habitat creation for both flora and fauna.

Oddly, much of the managed landscape that is often regarded as 'greenfield' comprises farmland that has seen very little other than monoculture for years. By contrast, brownfield sites often lie derelict long enough for nature to fight back quite well in such a context – establishing some intriguing pioneer habitats, for example, and demonstrating that such sites can actually contain more species and more diversity than ones identified as greenfield.

The key challenge for designers is to ensure that they maximise the potential for a rich and diverse landscape – seeking to improve on what was on the original site in terms of the number and diversity of species, whatever the inherited context.

As maintenance-free attitudes to landscapes and our love affair with the car prevail, there is a growing recognition that there are environmental, social and economic costs to the rapid increase in the hard surfaces that always accompany such trends. Initiatives such as SUDS (sustainable drainage systems) have sought to reverse this degradation. The opening (open space) is therefore there around and amongst us both for conserving existing habitats and for creating new ones.

Allotments, urban horticulture, productive gardens and rolling out the concept of edible landscapes, (including urban farms) offer exciting new opportunities.

The city of Berlin has a '50 per cent rule' for new developments, whereby half the built-up footprint of any site has to be biodiverse – it can be 'greenscape' (gardens, etc.) or 'bluescape' (ponds, etc.).

Whether it is holding on to the existing biodiversity of a site or creating new habitats, the Berlin 50 per cent rule of matching every m$^2$ of building with a m$^2$ of biodiverse landscape (also used at Malmö) is an exciting challenge.
Malmö City Council.
Photo Howard Liddell

# Design for Recycling:

Anything can be recycled, but at what cost? Easy recyclability is a sustainable design issue.

It has been mentioned in the section on 'recycled materials' (page 39), that there is nothing that cannot be recycled – given enough time and expense. However, as well as seeking economical ways of reusing processed materials and products that were manufactured without recycling in mind, we should also be learning from previous approaches to manufacture and assembly. This would encourage us once again to start manufacturing materials – and constructing buildings and landscapes – that can be readily reused, demounted, disassembled, eventually recycled and, ultimately, benignly disposed of back to the earth.

The benefits can be more than long term – demountability also affords flexibility in the short and medium term. Knowing that plumbers and electricians are going to want to get at pipes and wires, it seems obvious that we should make it easy for them to do so without having to wreck floors, walls and ceilings. As an example, 'nail-free' construction has been developed with this in mind. Lime mortar in brickwork allows a wall to be taken down without breaking the bricks; cement mortar, being stronger than the bricks it connects, necessitates smashing those bricks at demolition, as this is easier than breaking the mortar.

Given the trend of the last 30 years towards ever-shorter lifespans for buildings, it is alarming that our methods of building have embraced ever more permanent materials, products and construction systems.

A Shinto shrine is taken down and rebuilt every 20 years as a process of spiritual cleansing. Knowing this will happen affects the design.

**NailFree is a synthetic rubber based floor design.**
Gaia Architects, 2012. Photo Michael Wolchover

# Benign Materials

Only 3 per cent of the estimated 55,000 materials we currently use in buildings have been tested for their impact on human health.

Those pursuing a green design agenda often make assumptions about local materials being inherently a better choice than those from further afield. There is even a 'bioregional' movement.

The significance attributed to such materials appears to be (a) that they will contain less embodied energy in getting to the site and (b) that their purchase will contribute to the local economy.

Both of these assumptions can be challenged, however.

It is important to look at every material on its merit.

Due to a determination to produce its own windows for its own use Glasgow Council at one time manufactured its own – except that its chosen material was uPVC, a basic material with a very large carbon and water footprint before it ever reached the city for turning into windows.

If non-toxic paint is not manufactured locally, it is nevertheless important to have a benign indoor climate – and the latter should be an overriding consideration.

Once a building has been sealed up in the name of energy conservation it does not just need a policy of 'build tight, ventilate right'.

There are two key areas of concern which require mitigation; the first is material toxicity and the second is humidity. A sealed building needs to have materials internally that are both benign and open porous.

In general, ecological design decisions should not be made on the basis of a single criterion – good-quality eco-labelling is a sophisticated tool and should sit well beyond the ambit or influence of the simplistic rhetoric of product marketing.

Given a choice between a local product with questionable health credentials and a guaranteed healthy material that will perform the same function, most parents would not spend long making a decision about which to use for decorating their nursery.

Knowing the credentials of a material is essential for ecological specification. If the designer has not been party to the procurement cycle then third-party accreditation is necessary to ensure a healthy (non-toxic) indoor climate.

Glencoe, Gaia Architects. Photo Michael Wolchover

# Mass Timber:
## Huge potential impact in carbon sequestration.

Modern methods of mass-timber construction developed in Switzerland over the past two decades, and expanding from Central Europe to Scandinavia, have meant that low-grade timber can be brought into the building industry at rates competitive not just with other forms of timber construction but also with masonry and other heavyweight methods.

Even species such as Sitka spruce – of which there is an overabundance in the UK – can be brought into the construction industry through this technology, and perform in a way that was never before possible. For example, a 10 cm deep solid brettstapel (dowelled mass timber) plank can span up to 12 metres and can also act as a permanent, self-finished reinforcement platform for concrete.

This form of construction acts as a carbon-storage system and can be a major contributor, beyond mere carbon-neutral buildings, towards carbon-sink buildings. The chemical logic runs as follows: the $CO_2$ equivalent of 1 kg of wood-fixed carbon is about 3.6 kg, and, therefore, as seasoned wood is 50 per cent carbon, about 1.8 kg of $CO_2$ is bound into 1 kg of wood product.

This building material is pure eco-minimalism: contributing to good value for money, healthy indoor-climate credentials and a perfect strategy for carbon storage – and all invisible to the untutored eye.

One of the most promising (and most subtle) potential contributors to the carbon crunch is mass timber – which fixes 1.8 kg of $CO_2$ for every 1kg of timber. It takes the agenda way beyond the concept of a low-embodied-energy material to that of a carbon sponge.
Acharacle primary school. Gaia Architects.
Photo Howard Liddell

Calculations in Norway have indicated that a 'mode shift' from standard methods of construction to mass timber could have a more significant impact on reducing the country's carbon footprint than removing all the cars from the roads.

# Maintenance:
If something is to be sustainable, it must also be maintainable.

Given that the purchase of a building is often the largest single investment an individual will make, it is quite bizarre that the concept of buildings or building products being maintenance-free has gained credence. In stark contrast, it is regarded as a positive asset for a car to have a regular service record and it is written into the purchase agreement of electronic equipment. (Of course, there is something confidence-sapping in the offer of an extended warranty from one to three years that often costs half the price of the hardware being bought!)

Why would it be smart not to have an annual external-fabric check (gutter cleaning; check on roof, windows, doors; etc.)? All that a lack of maintenance does is allow a small problem to become a big one. This usually means that the repair and replacement cost of the big problem far outweighs the equivalent cost of regular maintenance.

Many building suppliers pride themselves on having a product that is maintenance-free and does not require painting. All too often, this means that they cannot be maintained and they cannot be painted.

Change is an intrinsic part of life and of living. People's social, financial and environmental circumstances are all constantly evolving and all require constant attention if they are to thrive.

Routine maintenance is an intrinsic part of good housekeeping and is an insurance against premature building-product or equipment replacement.

# WINDOW CLEANING
## UPVC Cleaning & Restoration

# GARDEN MAINTENANCE
## Grass Cutting          Hedge Trimming

This white van message rather undermines 25 years of marketing uPVC products – promoted as maintenance-free. Maybe the industry has realised that it is those products that cannot be maintained that are the real problem.

Photo Howard Liddell

Swiss hydro power. Photo Howard Liddell

# water

# element

# Water Conservation

As with energy strategies, it makes little sense, either economic or environmental, to concentrate on treatment and 'end-of-pipe' solutions before having ensured that everything possible has been done to reduce the load requiring end treatment.

Even in high rainfall regions, it is not the mere quantity of water being used, for example to flush WCs, that is the problem – it is the fact that this is usually potable (drinking quality) water, which has acquired an environmental and an economic cost en route to the supplying appliances. The proportion of water being used for flushing, bathing and washing clothes is nearly 60 per cent of an individual's daily demand in the UK.

Using dual-flush, low-flush, super-low-flush, waterless and other forms of conservation plumbing fittings, the reduction in both demand and treatment provision is dramatic and delivers both an environmental and an economic benefit.

Rainwater harvesting, grey-water recycling, composters, separating WCs and other intermediate technologies can also have an impact – but each needs to be reviewed on a project-specific basis, as it will be competing for budget with other environmental strategies.

The context within which decisions are being made on water conservation is in all cases the first point of reference.

Even in areas of high rainfall, it is not merely the amount of water but the amount of (bought) drinking-quality water – most of which is used for WC flushing – that is at issue.

Whilst the UK has been dragging its feet in producing eco-products, other Europeans have simply gone ahead and created their markets.  This low-flush WC uses rainwater.

W.C. Elemental Solutions. Photo Sandy Halliday

# Hard Surfaces:
## Rainwater – an opportunity.

Where hard surfaces are unavoidable, it is important to look at the resulting water run-off and retention. In terms of holding up the water flow, the principle of cleanliness prevails: any polluted water, such as the outflow from areas of car use, needs to be contained and not allowed to go to ground or pipes until properly trapped and filtered.

In terms of rainwater retention, the use of 'swales' – whereby the impact of periods of high rainfall is mitigated by the creation of temporary ponds – is now commonplace. Hard surfaces at roof level offer an opportunity for rainwater collection, as indeed do the elevations of high-rise buildings, which receive more rainfall than their relatively small roof areas by virtue of the fact that rain tends usually to fall at an angle to the vertical.

The use of retained water, or even water in the process of aeration, can offer amenity opportunities such as a water sculpture, waterfalls or ponds. The creative and artistic use of water is something that is much better understood and used in mainland Europe.

It is said that Birmingham has more canals than Venice (36 and 26 miles, respectively), but they are kept well hidden. However, the UK has developed a negative relationship with water. Those canals are so often littered with supermarket trolleys and plastic detritus and, unlike the Dutch, we have a tendency to want to fence them off rather than enjoy them, seeing them as a place for children to drown in rather than ensuring they are drawn to safer places where the water is appropriately shallow and inviting.

Water is also part of the designer's climatic modification toolbox, and can help to create successful microclimates – particularly in semi-contained spaces.

If we stopped putting water down drains and played with it in the open a little more, we would not only help address the increasing incidence of flooding – we would also make better public places.

To deal with rainwater run-off, we can use the sponge or the container. Where hard surfaces are unavoidable, they can be used to good effect as a context for water engineering, including sculpture.
Fairfield. Gaia Architects.
Photo Michael Wolchover

# Soft Surfaces

Soft surfaces are increasingly important as the UK addresses climate change and increased flooding. At high level, soft roofing retains water and delays its release into the surface water run-off system. The author's disparaging comments about turf roofs being an eco-cliché (see the section on green roofs on page 37) can be reviewed if consideration of a more lightweight and environmentally sound material base (e.g. sedum) roof can provide a genuine environmental benefit at little or no extra cost.

It can also achieve run-off delay and losses via evaporation. Feeding gardens from paths and other (non-polluted) run-off areas is also a potential mutual benefit arrangement.

## Car parking choices

Setting aside completely any discussion about congestion or pollution and focusing strictly on land-use issues, there is a discussion to be had about the motor car's impact in generating inordinate amounts of hard surface at ground level. There is a direct relationship between parking policy (e.g. currently two per household in Birmingham) and the impact on urban landscapes.

Centralised and/or stacked (e.g. in a 'paternoster' parking machine), car footprints can be reduced. The author has calculated – from a selection of low-density developments – that an average two-storey house with a single garage and a single parking space has roughly equal amounts of concrete (or equivalent) hard surface for both the house and the car. This includes a footpath for the pedestrians and the backing-out space and road requirements for the vehicle. In anything other than a very low-density scheme, the extent of residual area for soft landscaping will be minimal. Moving up to a double garage and two parking spaces virtually doubles the area needed for cars; in other words, the land requirement for cars is twice that required for people. Clearly, we are 'voting with our wheels'.

It is not possible to discuss the introduction of more soft surfaces without also addressing the issue of the motor car.

**Where soft surfaces are possible they should be the first choice. They usually need to make their case against the competing objective to cover the globe in asphalt.**

Rainwater run-off to gardens in Stroud co-ownership housing. Architype Architects.
Photo Howard Liddell

# Moisture Mass:
## Absorbent finishes are nine times better than mechanical ventilation at dealing with humidity.

We are used to thinking about thermal mass – we know that the sea holds onto heat during the summer. We also know that a clay-tiled floor will hold onto solar gain better than a carpeted one.

There is an equivalent phenomenon with moisture.

Contemporary construction has moved away from buildings which have walls, ceilings and floors made from natural, moisture-open (hygroscopic) materials – such as lime plaster, timber and mineral paints – to a palette of man-made, and usually impervious, materials and finishes such as chipboard, polyurethane-coated laminate floors, emulsion-sealed plasterboard and vinyl wallpapers and floor coverings.

This trend has led to an indoor moisture problem. The humidity in the air has nowhere to go and the levels rise – creating ideal conditions for dust mites and mould, which thrive above 60 per cent RH (relative humidity) – 100 per cent is a rainy day, whilst the middle of the Sahara is closer to zero (in the daytime). Humans are most comfortable around 40-60 per cent RH.

The tendency has been to counter this with increasing quantities of mechanical ventilation – often controlled by a 'humidostat' that triggers with high levels of RH. However, mechanical ventilation is a crude tool for removing moisture. Fans are efficient at moving air around – but the vapour in the air is less compliant. Indeed, according to recent Finnish research fans are nine times less effective than hygroscopic materials (untreated timber, unbaked clay, mineral-painted lime plaster, etc.) and they also take away lots of precious warm air. By using such materials, we can 'head off the problem at the pass' – giving a whole new meaning to the term 'passive' design.

Mechanical engineers can only work with what the architect gives them. If it is a glass box with impervious internal surfaces, they start on the back foot.

The classroom is made from mass-timber and clay-timer. These are examples of new-old traditional materials that work extremely well as indoor humidity dampers.
Architect. Gaia
Photo Gaia

# Capital Cost

'Buildings need to get greener faster
... to regard green buildings as special
may not help the cause.'[10]

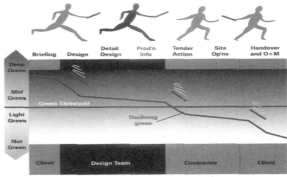

...Once dropped its is difficult to pick up again and regain lost ground

Green Baton. Diagram by Howard Liddell

### 'Read my lips'

The precepts of 'anti-bling', pro-common sense eco-minimalism must also challenge, head on, the fallacious assumption that it costs more in capital terms to build green. At client briefings and project meetings around the country, this false premise lingers and leads inevitably to discussions about how the unsubstantiated extra 'moolah' can be justified through reduced costs in use or life cycle costing benefits.

Even if I believed that such a debate was necessary – which I don't – it is rarely backed up with real evidence, and more rarely still does it result in an increased capital budget. Imagine the wasted effort and damage to relationships that accompany a fight to secure funding that, but for an eco-minimalist approach, might not actually be needed at all! It's an Alice in Wonderland world of shoddy thinking that has the net effect of stultifying any progress on the delivery of green buildings even before the ink is dry on project briefs.

Once commenced the possibility of maintaining (a) the cost plan to budget and (b) the specification reduces as the project progresses. At each stage the 'green baton' can be dropped and the further the project proceeds the more difficult it is to regain ground on both the cost and the specification. It is my assessment that over 95 per cent of well-meaning green briefs fail to deliver even tokenistic green buildings.

One thing is for certain, the technical-fix approach to green buildings will cost more – because it is additive. What has been added on can all too easily be taken off, and in the vast majority of cases that is exactly what will happen if (when) cost savings have to be achieved. It all starts with good green intentions, which then can't be afforded and so are ditched. Ironically given the poor performance – even in environmental terms – of most of the building-mounted technologies, the net result may actually end up with a lesser green footprint anyway.

Of course, it need not be like this. In the hands of an experienced eco-minimalist designer, the good-housekeeping approach will cost little or no more because it is inclusive; it has been designed in and not on.

### Let's say it again – it does not need to cost more

'Successful solutions result from "going for it" rather than worrying about the cost-effectiveness of every single item.'[11]

We are faced, however, with a conundrum. While the myth of 'going for it' being more expensive prevails, there is a simultaneous and unresolved question as to how 'going for it' might be defined.

There is a small amount of very useful work to inform this question – and all of it confirms one key thing: that well-researched green design can actually lead to buildings that cost less. Even when it leads to more costly buildings, the extra amount is so small as to

10 Bill Bordass, 'Cost and Value: Fact and Fiction'.
11 Ibid.

**The Cost of green buildings**

Chart compiled by Howard Liddell

| Study | Savings> 100% | Additional Cost %> |
|---|---|---|
| | 60% 70% 80% 90% | 100 101 103 104 105 106 107 108 109 110 |
| **LEED (1)** Schools+Offices | | <          > |
| **BREEAM** Domestic | | <  >      > |
| Offices | | <  >      |
| **Austrian e.g.** Ludesch centre | | > |
| **Gaia (Ind'l)** Rock bottom | > | |
| light green | > | |
| deep green | > | |
| **Gaia** Sports Centre | > | |
| Housing | > | |
| Vistor Centre | > | |
| **Solarbau** Datapec | > | |
| WAT | > | |
| Prisma | > | <Additional Cost of design |
| **LEED (2)** Academic (norm) | < > | |
| Academic (green) | < > | |
| Libraries(norm) | < > | |
| Libraries (green) | < > | |

be almost irrelevant. However, this information is not getting out into the public domain.

Without proper information, we are mired in a daunting combination of ignorance and prejudice. Hence the need for this book, and its message of eco-minimalism, which aims to demonstrate that, within reason and above a minimal quality threshold, building green need not cost more. Eco-minimalism is not necessarily easy to achieve – it requires an appropriately experienced designer to be able to make the trade-offs and be selective in specification and design – but it is possible.

Interestingly, over the 30 years of my practice producing only green buildings nobody ever gave us more money to build these for them, nor did we ask for it. We are not aware of any magic wand that has allowed us to do this in isolation from the so-called 'real world'.

### Whose definition?

The following is a selection of some of the studies that have been undertaken on the relative cost of building green.

### Labelled buildings

*For instance, BREEAM or LEED green building 'labels'.*

1 A feedback study by Cyril Sweett of BREEAM- and EcoHomes-assessed buildings demonstrated that improvements in their sustainability performance had been achieved at very little extra cost. It showed that achieving a 'good' rating in domestic projects increases the capital cost by a mere 0.5 per cent, and that for the 'excellent' rating the increase is more like 5 per cent. For offices, achieving a 'good' rating can marginally reduce the capital expenditure – and to reach an 'excellent' only requires adding 3 per cent.[12]

2 A similar study using the LEED assessment system – the US equivalent of BREEAM – showed a cost premium of 0.66 per cent ('certified') to 6.5 per cent ('platinum') for schools and offices.[13]

3 In the case of the £3 million town centre development in Ludesch, built in the Vorarlberg area of Austria in 2005, the clients commissioned a parallel study during the construction period to establish the additional cost of adopting a very high quality of passive design and a healthy building materials specification. The research report identified the additional costs for the whole project as being of the order of 3 per cent – and that for the vetted healthy-building materials (third-party reviewed by IBÖ, the Austrian Institute for Building Biology) to be a maximum of 1.9 per cent over conventional costs, with a cost-in-use benefit that paid for itself in the first few months of occupation. (This sum does not include the cost for the third-party vetting of the materials for their health credentials.) In looking at the nature of the materials used and their current availability in the UK, the percentage additional costs are transferable and equivalent to UK costs.[14]

12 Cyril Sweett, 'Putting a Price on Sustainability'.
13 Greg Kats, 'The Costs and Financial Benefits of Green Buildings', a report to California's Sustainable Building Task Force.
14 Wehinger, Torghele, Mötzl, et al. 'Neubau Ökologisches Gemeindezentrum Ludesch (New-build Ecological District Centre, Ludesch)'.

**4** The £2 million Glencoe Visitor Centre in the Scottish Highlands was built in 2002 and, by careful design and selection of materials (including home-grown timber; biomass fuel heating; natural ventilation; breathing floor, walls and roof construction; demountable (nail-free) detailing; new British slate roofing; low-flush WCs and waterless urinals) was delivered on a par with similar facilities in the UK. Its mechanical and electrical engineering content was reduced via a strategy of passive design, super-insulation and airtight construction to 9 per cent of the capital cost (as against a norm of around 25 per cent). The 16 per cent trade-off in unused heating, ventilation and electrical technology was used for the higher-quality fabric, including a high standard of healthy building materials. The healthy specification stipulated zero PVC, formaldehyde or VOC (volatile organic compound) content in materials. It included natural and untreated timber inside and out, mineral paints, cellulose fibre insulation, sheep's wool caulking around windows and linoleum floor covering. Unlike the Ludesch building work, no detailed analysis or third-party vetting of materials was undertaken. The above information has been derived from the architects and quantity surveyor.

### Solarbau Project

**5** In Germany, where the value of additional pre-construction indoor environmental design and modelling is appreciated and valued, it has been shown to save up to 25 per cent on capital construction costs.[15] In addition it has shown up to 50 per cent improvement in running costs when compared with equivalent conventional buildings.

The first three studies include buildings with add-ons (photovoltaics, small turbines, etc.), and it is evident that if an eco-minimalist approach had been adopted then all three would be reporting even lower figures. The introduction to the Cyril Sweett study says: "One of the principal barriers to [green] solutions is the perception that they incur substantial additional costs. This study contradicts this assumption."

"Estimation procedures can often be found wanting when looking at individual green features, which can be picked off one by one as not cost effective, whereas they would hang together as a package."

*Bill Bordass*

### Cost/m² studies

**1** A US study looked at a whole range of buildings with both green (i.e. LEED-rated) and non-green credentials, with costs ranging between £1,000 and £3,000 per m². Significantly, the buildings with green credentials appeared in every cost band – from 'cheap' to 'expensive'. In other words, the quality of the architecture was of far more significance, in cost terms, than whether the buildings were green or not.[16]

15 The Solarbau Initiative involved three mixed-use development projects, saving between 10 and 15 per cent on capital costs and up to 50 per cent on running costs – for an extra 1 per cent in fees.
16 Davis Langdon Adamson, 'Costing Green: A Comprehensive Cost Database and Budgeting Methodology'.

McLaren Centre.
Gaia Architects. Photo Howard Liddell

2 In a small study for an industrial eco-park for Scottish Enterprise, GAIA and their quantity surveyor colleagues investigated the additional cost, in low-budget industrial buildings, of constructing the units with a varying materials specification – from 'as cheap as possible', to 'light green' and, finally, 'deep green'. This study showed that at the lowest costs there was virtually nothing to trade off in order to build green. However, as the cost increased to a more reasonable (and average standard) budget, the trade-offs became possible. There is, therefore, a minimum cost benchmark, below which it is very difficult to build green – but it is indeed very low.[17]

3 In feedback audits on their own buildings, built between 1998 and 2003, GAIA managed to deliver projects with accredited 'high green' credentials at quite basic cost levels, i.e. with construction costs in a range between £800 and £1,750 per $m^2$ for leisure, residential and office buildings. All of these were at no more (and sometimes less) cost than contemporary, equivalent, non-green buildings built by others.[18]

### ... and benefits
### Work (economy), folk (community), place (environment)

Whilst lip service is paid to the equal importance of environmental, social and economic factors, the economic are always made 'more equal' than the others. Hence the need once and for all to nail the myth about the extra capital cost of building green

(see above).

Fortunately, the news gets better: once a green building has been delivered, it is win–win all over the place! Not only are costs in use lower than for equivalent non-green buildings, but there are plenty of other benefits too.

### Win–win for work

The financial benefits of green building include lower energy, waste disposal and water costs, lower environmental and emissions costs, lower operations and maintenance costs and savings from increased productivity and health. And in terms of refurbishment:

"An initial upfront investment of up to £50,000 to incorporate green building features into a £2.5 million project would result in savings of at least £500,000 over the life of the building, assumed conservatively to be 20 years."[19]

### Win–win for folk

Studies in the USA into healthy indoor-climate design and productivity have indicated dramatic reductions in:

- Acute respiratory illness (ARI) of 23–76 per cent (worth $6 bn to $14 bn per year in the USA).

- Allergies and asthma of 8–25 per cent (worth $6 bn to $14 bn per year in reduced health costs and $1 bn to $4 bn in economic gains).

17 Gaia and Ralph Ogg, 'Cost Study for Forfar Eco-park'.
18 Various GAIA in-house and commissioned third-party reports.
19 Greg Kats, op. cit.

Tollhouse Gardens. Gaia Architects. Photo Howard Liddell

- Sick building syndrome (SBS) of 20–25 per cent (worth $10 bn to $30 bn per year).

- Direct productivity gains of 0.5–5 per cent (worth $20 bn to $200 bn per year).[20]

There are UK examples – but they are not as comprehensive.

### Win–win for place

The above studies indicate direct gains to individual buildings and their users. However, these gains accrue to the benefit of whole economies, whole communities and the local, regional and global environments.

### Summary and conclusions

The skilled practitioners will trade off the higher price of certain sustainable materials by moving towards passive design and away from highly serviced buildings. They will do this by employing careful orientation, massing design and detailed specification. The use of passive design, breathing-wall construction, hygroscopic finishes, natural ventilation, the elimination of air conditioning and similar measures can all be used to reduce costs.

Such a strategy is, of course, going to be affected by the type of building in question. It should also be borne in mind that the initial cost of a building is relatively small in relation to its whole-life cost and, therefore, increased construction prices will not be particularly relevant over the life of the building unless they are of considerable magnitude. It is also necessary to consider costs holistically, as tertiary benefits (improved health, reduced absenteeism, etc.) will accrue to either the building owner or society as a whole – and ultimately both.

"Call a thing immoral or ugly, soul-destroying or a degradation of man, a peril to the peace of the world or to the well-being of future generations; as long as you have not shown it to be "uneconomic" you have not really questioned its right to exist, grow, and prosper."

*E. F. Schumacher*

20 William Fisk and Satish Kumar, 'Health and Productivity Gains From Better Indoor Environments'.

# Postscript

This excellent book is about the technologies, broadly considered, of the buildings we live and work in, the nature and amount of energy and materials they use, and their impact on the environment. Howard's proposals are invariably practical – he was brought up on the dictum that an ounce of practice is worth a ton of theory – and some demand big changes in the value judgements and decisions of architects and builders and of policy-makers. In a world of escalating oil prices and impending shortages of supply, and where climate change is starting to make itself felt, it is imperative that the kind of research and analysis that make this book so compelling are continued.

I was fortunate enough to have Fritz Schumacher as a friend and colleague during much of my working life, and especially during two spells of work that involved the promotion of widespread changes in technology. The first was when we formed the Intermediate Technology Development Group (now renamed Practical Action) in 1964, to promote the use of small-scale, inexpensive, labour-using machines and equipment. The prevailing practice of aid-givers, now largely discredited, was to lumber poor countries with the labour-saving, high-cost technology of the rich countries. We largely succeeded in our aim, as Practical Action is now well known internationally, is working with partner bodies in six developing countries and runs a successful consulting company and information service. We were also involved with the Soil Association, which was started in 1946 and is now a leading environmental charity campaigning for the global shift of agriculture to organic, sustainable food and farming.

Both Practical Action and the Soil Association are now influential bodies with international reputations. Both have the support of research and consultancy organisations; both publish journals and undertake educational work. At the time when they were first formed, both were either ignored or considered eccentric or plain cranky. Today they are highly regarded, except by eccentrics and cranks. I am surely not alone in believing that Howard could now create an organisation much needed by architects and builders which could quickly become as effective in its field as Practical Action and the Soil Association are in theirs. It could, to take some examples, publicise and promote best practice and pillory the worst; update knowledge of relevant research and fill gaps in knowledge by doing or commissioning research; identify issues requiring legislation, or changes in professional skills; publish material for small builders and for the public at large, or for informing clients; provide relevant material for the training of architects and builders. Its motto might be: 'An ounce of better practice is worth a ton of theory.'

**George McRobie**
February 2013

# References/ Selected Reading

## References

**Carson, R.** (1962) *Silent Spring*. Houghton Mifflin Company.

**Dickson, D.** (1974) *Alternative Technology and the Politics of Technical Change*. Fontana.

**Geddes, P.** (1931) *Sciences in General*. Life.

**Halliday, S.** (2008) *Sustainable Construction*. Butterworth Heinemann.

**Halliday, S.** (2000) *Green Guide to the Architect's Job Book*. RIBA Publications.

**Liddell, H.** (2006) *Eco-minimalism, Green Building Bible Volume 1*. Green Building Press, pp 98–103.

**Patterson, W.** (1976) *The Energy Alternative: Changing the Way the World Works*. Available from http://www. waltpatterson.org/contents.htm

**Schmid, P.** (1986) *Bio-logische Baikonstruktion*. Rudolph Müller.

**Schumacher, E.F.** (1973) *Small is Beautiful. A Study of Economics as if People Mattered*. Blond Briggs.

**Schumacher, E.F.** (1979) *Good Works*. Jonathan Cape.

**Seymour, J. and S.** (1970) *Self-Sufficiency*. Faber & Faber.

**Steingraber, S.** (1997) *Living Downstream*. Virago Press.

**Vale, B. and R.** (1975) *The Autonomous House*. Thames and Hudson.

**McRobie, G.** (1981) *Small is Possible*. Jonathan Cape.

### Four elements

**Berge, B.** (1999) *The Ecology of Building Materials*. Architectural Press.

**Halliday, S. and Morrison, C.** (2003) *Children's Eco City Project*. Children's Parliament.

### Eco-bling

**BEAMA** *(British Electrotechnical and Allied Manufacturers Association)* (2007) *Metering and Monitoring of Domestic Embedded Generation*. House of Commons (28 November 2007).

**Danmarks Tekniske Universitet** (DTU) (2005) *Moisture Buffering of Building Materials: Report BYG-EDTU R-126*. Department of Civil Engineering, Technical University of Denmark.

**Jaakkola, J.J., Verkasalo, P.K. and Jaakkola, N.** (2000) *Plastic wall materials in the home and respiratory health in young children*. American Journal of Public Health 90: 797–799.

**Liddell, H., Kay, T. and Stevenson, F.** (1993) *Recycled Materials for Housing*. Scottish Homes.

**London Hazards Centre** (1989) *Toxic Treatments*.

**Norton, B.** (2000) *Heating Water by the Sun*. Centre for Alternative Technology.

**Oreszczyn, T.** *Energy Efficiency in the UK*. Presented at Royal Institution, Glasgow, 15 February 2006.

### Eco-minimalism

**Dreiseitl, H., Grau, D. and Ludwig, K.** (2003) *Waterscapes: Planning, Building and Designing with Water*. Birkhauser.

**Environment Agency/SEPA.** Designs that hold water – Sustainable Urban Drainage Systems explained. Video (undated), www. sepa.org.uk

**Feynman. R. P.** (1985) *Surely You're Joking, Mr. Feynman!* W. W. Norton.

**Gaia Architects** (2003) *Light Earth Construction*. Gaia Research.

**Gaia Group** (2005) *Design and Construction of Sustainable Schools, Vols 1 and 2*. Scottish Executive.

**Grant, N., Moodie, M. and Weedon, C.** (1996) *Sewage Solutions*. Centre for Alternative Technology.

**Halliday, S.P., Chapman, B., Jones, P. and Liddell, H.L.** (2005) *Affordable Low Allergy Housing*. Gaia Research.

**Houben, H. and Guillard, H.** (1994) *Earth Construction*. Intermediate Technology.

**Pejtersen, J., Øie, L., Skar, S., Clausen, G. and Fanger, P.O.** (1990) *A simple method to determine the olf load in a building*. Proceedings of 5th International Conference on Indoor Air Quality and Climate, Indoor Air '90. Toronto, Canada, Vol. 1, pp. 537–42.

**Roalkvam, D.** (1997) *Naturlig Ventilasjon* NABU/NFR (in Norwegian).

**SEDA Design Guides: 1.** Design and Detailing for Airtightness. 2. Design and Detailing for Deconstruction. 3. Design and Detailing for Toxic Chemical Reduction in Buildings. Available from http://www.seda.uk.net/design_guides.html

One Watt standby http://www.iea.org/textbase/papers/2005/standby_fact.

pdfPassivhaus

## Cost

**Bordass, B.**(2000) Cost and value: fact and fiction. Building Research and Information Volume 28, Numbers 5-6, 1 September 2000, pp. 338–352.

**BRE Centre for Sustainable Construction, BRE Trust and Sweett, C.** (2005) *Putting a Price on Sustainability.*

**Greg, K. et al.** (2003) The Costs and Financial Benefits of Green Buildings: A Report to California's Sustainable Building Task Force.

**Lovins, A.L. and von Weizacher, E.** (1997) *Factor 4 – Doubling Wealth and Halving Resources.* Earthscan.

**Matthiesson, L. and Morris, P.** (2004) Costing Green: A Comprehensive Cost Database & Budgeting Methodology. Davis Langdon Adamson.

**Wehinger, Torghele, G. Mötzl, et al.** (2006) *Neubau ökologisches Gemeindezentrum Ludesch.* Bundesministerium fur Verkehr, Innovation + Technologie.

**William, F.J.** (2000) *Health and Productivity Gains from Better Indoor Environments and Their Relationship with Building Efficiency.* Annual Review of Energy and the Environment, Vol. 25, pp. 537–66.